BRINGING BACK THE

Blue Iguana

Ruth Daly

Crabtree Publishing Company
www.crabtreebooks.com

CRABTREE
PUBLISHING COMPANY
WWW.CRABTREEBOOKS.COM

Author: Ruth Daly

Series Research and Development: Reagan Miller

Picture Manager: Sophie Mortimer

Design Manager: Keith Davis

Editorial Director: Lindsey Lowe

Children's Publisher: Anne O'Daly

Editor: Ellen Rodger

Proofreader: Crystal Sikkens

Cover design: Margaret Amy Salter

Production coordinator and
    Prepress technician: Margaret Amy Salter

Print coordinator: Katherine Berti

Produced for Crabtree Publishing Company
by Brown Bear Books

Photographs

(t=top, b= bottom, l=left, r=right, c=center)

Front Cover: All images from Shutterstock

Interior: Alamy: Danita Delimont 25, Nature Picture Library 18, Timothy M. O'Keefe 8; Cayman Compass: Christopher Fletcher 20; CaymANNature: 21b; Shurna Decau 17t: Dreamstime: Deborah Coles 21t, Sandra Foyt 22, Tara Nylaka 15b; Floridaiguana.com: 15t; Getty Images: Flavio Vallenari 19c; iStock: Patrick Gijsbers 27b, Global Pics 26, Grafissimo 19b, josejuanfotos 7, Kirin Photo 28, Ken Wiedemann 14; Joan Maurer: 13; Nature Picture Library: Roland Seitre 10, 12, 13b, 16, 23; Public Domain: Tim Felce (Airwolfhound) 6, Pete Markham 9t, Kunal Mukherjee 9b; Shutterstock: 29, John E. Anderson 4, Frontpage 1, Jimcatlinphotography 5b, May-Lana 5t, Dennis Stewart 27t; South Florida Sun-Sentinel: Mike Stocker 24; TOTI Media, Inc: Glenn Ostle 17b.

Brown Bear Books has made every attempt to contact the copyright holder. If you have any information please contact licensing@brownbearbooks.co.uk

Library and Archives Canada Cataloguing in Publication

Title: Bringing back the blue iguana / Ruth Daly.
Names: Daly, Ruth, 1962- author.
Series: Animals back from the brink.
Description: Series statement: Animals back from the brink | Includes index.
Identifiers: Canadiana (print) 20190233435 | Canadiana (ebook) 20190233443 | ISBN 9780778768104 (hardcover) | ISBN 9780778768241 (softcover) | ISBN 9781427124258 (HTML)
Subjects: LCSH: Iguanas—Cayman Islands—Grand Cayman Island—Juvenile literature. | LCSH: Iguanas—Conservation—Cayman Islands—Grand Cayman Island—Juvenile literature. | LCSH: Endangered species—Cayman Islands—Grand Cayman Island—Juvenile literature. | LCSH: Wildlife recovery—Cayman Islands—Grand Cayman Island—Juvenile literature.
Classification: LCC QL666.L25 D35 2020 | DDC j597.95/420972921—dc23

Library of Congress Cataloging-in-Publication Data

Names: Daly, Ruth, 1962- author.
Title: Bringing back the Blue iguana / Ruth Daly.
Other titles: Animals back from the brink.
Description: New York, New York : Crabtree Publishing Company, [2020] | Series: Animals back from the brink | Includes index.
Identifiers: LCCN 2019053197 (print) | LCCN 2019053198 (ebook) | ISBN 9780778768104 (hardcover) | ISBN 9780778768241 (paperback) | ISBN 9781427124258 (ebook)
Subjects: LCSH: Iguanas--Conservation--Cayman Islands--Grand Cayman Island--Juvenile literature. | Wildlife conservation--Cayman Islands--Grand Cayman Island--Juvenile literature.
Classification: LCC QL666.L25 D35 2020 (print) | LCC QL666.L25 (ebook) | DDC 597.95/42--dc23
LC record available at https://lccn.loc.gov/2019053197
LC ebook record available at https://lccn.loc.gov/2019053198

Crabtree Publishing Company

www.crabtreebooks.com   1-800-387-7650

Printed in the U.S.A./022020/CG20200102

Published in Canada
Crabtree Publishing
616 Welland Ave.
St. Catharines, Ontario
L2M 5V6

Published in the United States
Crabtree Publishing
PMB 59051
350 Fifth Avenue, 59th Floor
New York, New York 10118

Published in the United Kingdom
Crabtree Publishing
Maritime House
Basin Road North, Hove
BN41 1WR

Published in Australia
Crabtree Publishing
Unit 3–5 Currumbin Court
Capalaba
QLD 4157

Contents

On the Brink of Extinction

The blue iguana, or Grand Cayman blue iguana, is a large lizard. It has red eyes, a spiky **crest**, and a long tail. Adult iguanas have blue-gray skin that helps to **camouflage** it in dry, rocky forests. Thousands of blue iguanas once lived on Grand Cayman, but about 300 years ago human settlers began to arrive. They brought dogs, cats, and rats with them, which soon became the iguanas' main **predators**. Houses, roads, and tourist facilities were built on the land where blue iguanas lived. By 2002, there were fewer than 20 blue iguanas living in the wild. Their population was so small it was very difficult for them to breed successfully enough for the **species** to survive. A survey that year declared the blue iguana to be **functionally extinct** in the wild.

Blue iguanas change color throughout the day. In the morning, when temperatures are cooler, their skin is gray. During the day, blue iguanas sit in hot, sunny places. As they warm up, their skin becomes brighter blue. In May, when they are looking for mates, their skin turns bright blue and then vivid turquoise.

BLUE IGUANA BASICS

Blue iguanas are **herbivores**. They can grow to about 5 feet (1.5 m) in length and weigh up to 25 pounds (11 kg). Their skin is thick and scaly, and a floppy flap of skin called a dewlap hangs below the throat. Their strong, sharp claws are used for digging, and they also have strong teeth and jaws. Blue iguanas have a crest of small spines from head to tail. These help to protect them from predators.

Like other lizards, blue iguanas are cold-blooded. They become hot or cold depending on the air temperature. Blue iguanas spend time warming up in the Sun before they become active. They can live for between 25 and 40 years in the wild. The oldest captive iguana lived to be 69 years old.

Blue iguanas are found only on Grand Cayman island. This is the largest of the three Cayman Islands lying to the southwest of Cuba. Before they became endangered, there were blue iguana populations on or near the beaches. Females laid their eggs in the sand. Now, most populations are inland.

Species at Risk

Created in 1984, the International Union for the Conservation of Nature (IUCN) protects wildlife, plants, and natural resources around the world. Its members include about 1,400 governments and nongovernmental organizations. The IUCN publishes the Red List of Threatened Species each year, which tells people how likely a plant or animal species is to become **extinct**. It began publishing the list in 1964.

SCIENTIFIC CRITERIA

The Red List, created by scientists, divides nearly 80,000 species of plants and animals into nine categories. Criteria for each category include the growth and decline of the population size of a species. They also include how many individuals within a species can breed, or have babies. In addition, scientists include information about the **habitat** of the species, such as its size and quality. These criteria allow scientists to figure out the probability of extinction facing the species.

Père David's Deer lived in China. The IUCN Red List classified it as Extinct in the Wild (EW) in 2008. A small captive population exists in China and there are hopes that it will be reintroduced to the wild.

IUCN LEVELS OF THREAT

The Red List uses nine categories to define the threat to a species.

Extinct (EX)	No living individuals survive.
Extinct in the Wild (EW)	Species cannot be found in its natural habitat. Exists only in captivity, in cultivation, or in an area that is not its natural habitat.
Critically Endangered (CR)	At extremely high risk of becoming extinct in the wild.
Endangered (EN)	At very high risk of extinction in the wild.
Vulnerable (VU)	At high risk of extinction in the wild.
Near Threatened (NT)	Likely to become threatened in the near future.
Least Concern (LC)	Widespread, abundant, or at low risk.
Data Deficient (DD)	Not enough data to make a judgment about the species.
Not Evaluated (NE)	Not yet evaluated against the criteria.

In the United States, the Endangered Species Act of 1973 was passed to protect species from possible extinction. It has its own criteria for classifying species, but they are similar to those of the IUCN. Canada introduced the Species at Risk Act in 2002. More than 530 species are protected under the act. The list of species is compiled by the Committee on the Status of Endangered Wildlife in Canada (COSEWIC).

IGUANAS AT RISK

Iguanas are one of the most endangered species. Their protection is vital for the health of the **ecosystem**, as iguanas are important seed dispersers for native plants. Many of the world's iguanas are Endangered (EN), Critically Endangered (CR), or Vulnerable (VU) on the IUCN Red List. The Navassa rhinoceros iguana was declared Extinct (EX) in 2011. In 2004, the blue iguana was listed as Critically Endangered (CR), but in 2012 this was upgraded to Endangered (EN).

Threats to Survival

In 1503, the explorer Christopher Columbus discovered the Cayman Islands. He noted the abundance of turtles and iguanas. Although pirates made the islands their base in the 1660s, Grand Cayman remained uninhabited until the mid-1700s. The new settlers cleared the land for houses and roads, and the iguanas were forced to move inland from their natural coastal habitat. As the human population increased, more land was cleared. Farmers replaced fruit trees with cattle pastures, which removed an important food source for the iguanas. Their habitat became **fragmented**. By the 1930s, blue iguanas were scarce. In the 1950s, the first airfield was opened on Grand Cayman, paving the way for increasing human development.

Grand Cayman is a popular place for people to spend time on vacation. A road was built all the way around the island to make travel easier. Blue iguanas also used the road because the warm tarmac was an ideal place to sunbathe. Unfortunately, many iguanas were run over as they were not fast enough to move out of the way of the traffic.

NATIVE PREDATORS

Snakes were the only predators of blue iguanas before the arrival of people. The Cayman Racer is a native snake that preys on young iguanas. **Hatchlings** can be about 8 inches (20 cm) long. Although they move fast, they are too small to defend themselves. Cayman Racers also steal iguana eggs from nests. As a result, many blue iguanas were killed before they reached breeding age.

IMPORTED PREDATORS

House building and land clearance were not the only threats to the blue iguana when people arrived on Grand Cayman. Dogs, cats, and rats arrived with them. At first, dogs and cats were kept as pets, but in some cases owners stopped caring for them and the animals became **feral**. In the wild, feral dogs and cats survive alone and are not tame like pets. Dogs kill iguanas of all sizes. Feral cats prey on hatchlings and small iguanas. Brown Norway rats dig up iguana nests looking for eggs or hatchlings. Blue iguanas had no natural fear of these animals because they were new to the island. The iguanas did not try to run away or hide, and were killed. The blue iguana population grew smaller. By the 1990s, conservationists realized that they must take action before the blue iguana became extinct.

Balancing the Ecosystem

Fossils of blue iguanas have been found on the beaches of Grand Cayman, indicating they must have lived near the coast for thousands of years. With the arrival of settlers in the 1700s, the iguanas moved to areas of scrubland inland. Blue iguanas played a critical role in seed **dispersal**. Their diet consisted of leaves, stems, fruit, and flowers from cacti and other plants. Fruit seeds passed through their digestive system and were deposited in the soil through their waste. The seeds grew into new plants, providing fresh food and shelter for the iguanas and other wildlife on the island. Although there are fewer blue iguanas today, they still play an important role in maintaining the balance of the ecosystem.

Inland, blue iguanas live in tree cavities or holes in rocks, in areas close to farms, roads, gardens, and forests. They eat fruit and flowers and dig their nests in soft soil, where they lay between 3 and 21 eggs.

INVASIVE SPECIES

An invasive species is a living thing introduced, usually by humans, to an area where it is not native, or does not naturally occur. Typically, an invasive species will cause harm to its new environment. They are a problem for **native species** because they can often become predators or destroy natural vegetation. Islands are most at risk from invasive species because they can lead to native species becoming extinct. Many countries have strict laws to prevent visitors from bringing in certain foods, plants, and animals. An invasive species that caused problems for blue iguanas were green iguanas. They were first noticed on Grand Cayman in the 1980s. They quickly threatened blue iguanas because they can lay 50 to 60 eggs at a time and eat large amounts of leaves, fruits, and flowers.

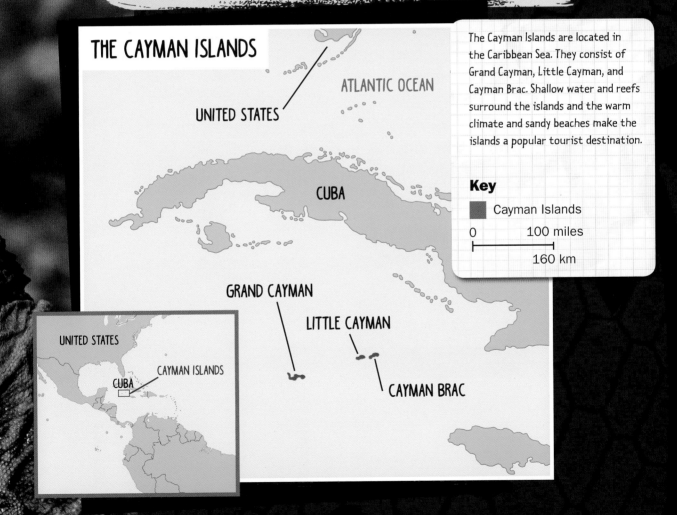

THE CAYMAN ISLANDS

ATLANTIC OCEAN

UNITED STATES

CUBA

GRAND CAYMAN

LITTLE CAYMAN

CAYMAN BRAC

UNITED STATES

CAYMAN ISLANDS

CUBA

The Cayman Islands are located in the Caribbean Sea. They consist of Grand Cayman, Little Cayman, and Cayman Brac. Shallow water and reefs surround the islands and the warm climate and sandy beaches make the islands a popular tourist destination.

Key

Cayman Islands

0   100 miles

160 km

Plan of Action

The **natural scientist** Frederic Burton is someone who wanted to make a difference. He moved to Grand Cayman in 1979, and worked as a **volunteer** for the National Trust. He was involved with many conservation projects, including taking a **census** to count the number of blue iguanas in the wild. He only found 25 and knew urgent action was needed. In the wild, blue iguana eggs hatch after about 10 weeks and the hatchlings all leave the nest together. This is when they are most likely to be eaten by snakes and feral cats. To try to save the species, Burton initially created a program to breed blue iguanas in captivity at his home. Since that time, he has raised funds and spoken up for important conservation issues that affect the Cayman Islands. Burton's breeding program was called the Blue Iguana Recovery Program (BIRP).

Frederic Burton moved the breeding program to the Queen Elizabeth II Botanic Park (QEII), which he launched with the help of donations in 1997. The park has 65 acres (26 ha) of land that includes wetlands, forests, ponds, flower gardens, and nature trails.

COLLABORATING FOR A CAUSE

When the Blue Iguana Recovery Program was founded in 1990, the goal was to release 1,000 blue iguanas into the wild. Several conservation groups from around the world helped by raising funds and sending vets and volunteers to work with the iguanas. One such volunteer was Joan Maurer, a veterinary technician at Milwaukee County Zoo. While she was at QEII, she collaborated with other vets and researchers. She used her medical and research skills to monitor the health of the blue iguanas. Some of her work involved carrying out health checks and photographing iguanas. Maurer was supported by The Wildlife Conservation Society based in New York. The Durrell Wildlife Conservation Trust and the International Reptile Conservation Society also helped to fund projects with the recovery program at various times.

A blue iguana egg and hatchling at the QEII Botanic Park. Burton's program involved collecting eggs from around the island and keeping them warm artificially so they could hatch in safety.

Breeding Program

Breeding blue iguanas in captivity protects them from predators. BIRP keeps the iguanas for at least two years until they became too big to be prey for cats and snakes, although feral dogs can still be a problem. After two or three years, the iguanas are released into protected nature **reserves** to live and breed in the wild. In the captive breeding program, iguana eggs are kept warm and moist in **incubators** for between 66 to 90 days. Hatchlings weigh about 2 ounces (57 g) when first born. They are fed on local plants, flowers, and berries until they are ready for release into the wild.

Some blue iguanas from the recovery program are sent to zoos in other countries. This is to ensure the survival of other populations in case diseases or natural disasters wipe out the population on Grand Cayman.

IGUANA WISH LIST

BIRP identified everything that the blue iguanas need to survive:

- Warmth and sunshine so their body temperature can reach 100°F (37.8°C)

- Fresh food and a small amount of water

- Soft soil where they can dig down to a least 12 inches (30 cm) to make their nests

- Rocky areas and hollow trees to provide shelter at night, as well as safe areas to hide from predators

- Other blue iguanas in sufficient numbers for each individual to find a mate and breed successfully

In the United States, the Phoenix Zoo Arizona Center for Nature Conservation is home to more than 3,000 animals, including many species that are endangered or threatened. The center has 126 species of reptiles, including the Grand Cayman blue iguana.

Saving the Blue Iguana

The blue iguana hatchlings born in captivity have to be separated from each other before they are a month old. At about this time they begin to act aggressively toward one another. Each iguana has its own cage where it does not have to compete for food with the other iguanas. Snakes are often spotted around hatchling cages. Volunteers and wardens check every day to make sure the cages are snake-proof.

By the time the young blue iguanas are about a year old, they start to spend time in trees and shrubs around the **enclosure**. They learn how to create small territories for themselves. Blue iguanas are ready to be released into the wild when they are about two years old. Breeding usually begins when they are between two and three years old.

Blue iguanas injured in the wild are taken to QEII for treatment. Sometimes they can be released back into the wild. The National Trust makes sure that old iguanas, and those too sick to be returned to the wild, are looked after in conditions as close to their natural habitat as possible.

INDIVIDUAL IGUANA "ID"

The **scales** and bumps on blue iguanas' faces make unique patterns. No two iguanas have the same markings, but it is not easy to tell them apart at first glance. Researchers have other ways to identify them. Microchips are inserted under the skin. This helps conservationists keep accurate records of the health of each iguana. Colored beads are also threaded through each iguana's crest. Some iguanas are given names to match the beads—for example, "Yog" might be named for a row of yellow, orange, and green beads.

COLLABORATING FOR A CAUSE

The original captive breeding **facility** at the QEII Botanic Park had several large cages and an open enclosure with secure fences. BIRP started by breeding between 10 and 20 hatchlings each year, but this grew to over 100. Grants from the World Wildlife Fund and other conservation groups helped QEII to buy more than 100 cages for **juveniles**, hatchlings, and adults. Wardens look after the iguanas, releasing 40 to 60 into the wild each year.

Salina Reserve, a rocky area of shrubland in the east of Grand Cayman. The land is owned and protected by the National Trust. Hidey boxes were placed in the reserve for the newly released iguanas to use as shelters from predators. The recovery program was so successful that after a few years there was not enough land to support all the blue iguanas at Salina. Another safe area needed to be found. In 2010, the National Trust purchased the Colliers Wilderness Reserve, a 190-acre (77 ha) site next to the Salina Reserve.

The Salina Reserve and Colliers Wilderness Reserve feature dry forests and shrubland that was typical all over Grand Cayman before people arrived. The reserves provide the ideal habitat for the blue iguana and a number of endangered bird species, including the Critically Endangered (CR) Grand Cayman parrot.

DANGEROUS DOGS

Although Salina and Colliers Wilderness are protected areas, feral dogs are still a danger. Dog owners are required by law to keep them on leashes, but they sometimes escape. Small packs of dogs roam parts of the island and although the wardens set traps, there are too many dogs to catch them all. The breeding center at QEII is protected by fences, but if dogs find their way in, the blue iguanas roaming the trails become easy prey. In 2008, vandals broke into the QEII reserve with dogs. Seven iguanas died. Security was immediately improved with a high fence, razor wire, and security cameras.

GREEN IGUANA INVASION

Thousands of green iguanas live on Grand Cayman. They arrived after Hurricane Ivan in 2004, when areas of the island needed to be replanted. It is thought that green iguana hatchlings were inside containers of plants and grasses that were shipped in from Central America. Green iguanas are pests. They eat birds' eggs, huge amounts of flowers, trees, and crops, and dig burrows that damage roads. As a result, people began to kill green iguanas. Blue iguanas were also killed when people failed to recognize them.

Back from the Brink!

Over a period of about 20 years, the captive breeding program and the creation of protected areas had worked. Hatchlings were living in safety and growing to breeding age. The collaboration between BIRP and its many partners was successful in bringing blue iguanas back from the brink of extinction. From fewer than 25 in 2005, the blue iguana population grew to 750 in 2012. As a result, blue iguanas were **downgraded** by the IUCN from Critically Endangered (CR) to Endangered (EN). By 2019, BIRP—renamed the National Trust Blue Iguana Conservation Program—had released over 1,000 blue iguanas into the wild.

On July 23, 2018, the Blue Iguana Recovery Program released the 1,000th blue iguana into the wild. The iguana, named Renegade, was one of ten iguanas released into Colliers Wilderness Reserve. BIRP's original goal had been achieved.

EDUCATION

BIRP worked with schools on Grand Cayman to make them aware of how the blue iguana was saved from extinction. Children learned about conservation through games and activities, and visited the captive breeding center. The local curriculum was also modified to include conservation issues, with a special focus on blue iguanas. BIRP also set up a program to help people tell the difference between blue and green iguanas.

Fred Burton is shown here on the far left with experts at the Colliers Wilderness Reserve entrance in November 2016. Colliers Wilderness was funded by money from the European Union. A nature trail was created through the reserve, which contains native plants, birds, and butterflies, as well as the endangered blue iguana.

Blue Iguana Tourism

Making people aware of blue iguana conservation is an important part of the recovery program. Increased local awareness of the iguana raises much-needed funds for the program. Blue iguanas are one of the main tourist attractions on Grand Cayman. Many tourists also enjoy looking for the 15 blue iguana sculptures that have been placed around the island. Although there are benefits from tourism, one downside with having more tourists is increased traffic, and that leads to **roadkill**. Blue iguanas often sit next to roads and are accidentally hit by cars. This happens more often when iguanas move to new areas away from the reserves looking for suitable mates or searching for nesting grounds.

Rum Point Beach, on the north side of the island, is a popular tourist spot. Although tourists are good for the economy of Grand Cayman, more tourists means more dangers for the struggling population of blue iguanas.

COLLABORATING FOR A CAUSE

Part of Fred Burton's original plan was to have small populations of blue iguanas living at zoos around the world. Some zoos in the United States, such as the Indianapolis Zoo in Indiana, right, are part of the captive breeding program. Hatchlings have also been born at the Central Florida Zoo, and Bronx Zoo. Breeding blue iguanas at zoos outside Grand Cayman helps to make the species stronger because it increases their **genetic diversity** and increases public awareness.

GRAND CAYMAN ISLAND

GRAND CAYMAN

RUM POINT BEACH

SALINA RESERVE

QUEEN ELIZABETH II
BOTANIC PARK

COLLIERS
WILDERNESS
RESERVE

GEORGE TOWN

CARIBBEAN SEA

Blue iguanas currently live in three protected areas on Grand Cayman: Queen Elizabeth II Botanic Park, Colliers Wilderness Reserve, and Salina Reserve.

Key

0   5 miles

8 km

Looking to the Future

The green iguana population doubles every year. By 2018, there were approximately 1.5 million green iguanas on Grand Cayman. Blue and green iguanas share the same habitat. However, blue iguanas were seriously outnumbered and unable to compete for nesting sites and food. In 2018, the government of Grand Cayman announced a **cull** of green iguanas. The government hoped that this would help the blue iguanas, as well as the natural environment that was being destroyed by green iguanas. The target for 2019 was to reduce the green iguana population by 1.3 million. The target for 2020 was set lower. However, it is expected that as their numbers are reduced, they will be harder to find.

Before 2010, it was illegal to kill any type of iguana. This law was to protect blue iguanas but it also protected green iguanas. In 2018, United States' wildlife agencies in Florida gave citizens the right to kill green iguanas when they began to overrun neighborhoods and homes.

FUTURE THREATS

Seventeen blue iguanas died at QEII between 2015 and 2017. They were killed by an illness caused by a **bacteria** called helicobacter. This is naturally found in iguanas, but usually only at low levels that do not cause health problems. Some scientists thought the bacteria came from green iguanas, but this was never proven. Blue iguanas are regularly checked for signs of illness so that future outbreaks can be spotted early. Habitat destruction by natural disasters such as hurricanes, right, and forest fires are other threats to the iguanas. Conservationists from the recovery program currently take a survey once a year to count the wild population.

COLLABORATING FOR A CAUSE

The Blue Iguana Conservation Program's captive breeding centers depend on funding to pay salaries, buy equipment, and to keep the facilities in good condition. In 2019, The National Trust received a grant of over $200,000 from the Darwin Plus Initiative, which is a conservation group based in Great Britain that helps to protect natural environments around the world. The grant means that research and conservation projects can continue. More facilities can be built to house blue iguanas, and more staff can be employed to monitor them. The grant will also fund research into preventing diseases and solving the problem of predator attacks on wild iguanas.

Saving Other Species

The populations of many iguana species throughout the world are threatened by invasive species, the construction of roads and buildings, and habitat destruction. Conservationists hope that by adopting the methods that helped to save the blue iguana, they will be able to save other iguanas from joining the Navassa rhinoceros iguana on the IUCN Red List of Extinct (EX) species.

The Sister Isles rock iguana, also known as the Lesser Caymans iguana, has a total population of about 900 individuals. In 2012, it was classified as being Critically Endangered (CR) on the IUCN Red List.

Before the 1940s, there were thousands of Sister Isles rock iguanas on the islands of Little Cayman and Cayman Brac. Since then, their numbers have fallen and they are on the brink of extinction.

THE FIJI BANDED IGUANA

Since the 1990s, the population of Fiji banded iguanas has halved, and on some islands has become extinct. It is now only found on a handful of islands and the population is falling. This decline is due to loss of forest habitat due to mining, farming, and logging. An invasive species of mongoose also preys on them. There are thought to be around 4,000 to 6,000 remaining. In 2012, the IUCN Red List classified them as Endangered (EN).

UTILA SPINY-TAILED IGUANA

The Utila spiny-tailed iguana is found on the Caribbean island of Honduras. It has a population of between 3,000 and 6,000, which has declined as the tourist industry has grown. The construction of buildings, garbage dumps, and marinas have destroyed the mangrove forests where the iguanas live. Pollution from landfills, pesticides, and plastic garbage on the beaches, as well as invasive plant species, have all had a negative effect on the iguana. As well as the usual predators, Utila spiny-tailed iguanas are preyed upon by local people, who harvest the iguanas and their eggs and sell them. In 2018, the IUCN Red List classified the Utila spiny-tailed iguana as Critically Endangered (CR).

What Can You Do to Help?

The blue iguana is back from the brink of extinction, thanks to the work of dedicated people like Fred Burton. However, the blue iguana is far from safe. Even the smallest threats can harm the population. You may think there is nothing you can do to help the natural world and the animals and plants that we depend on for survival. However, simple changes of our behaviors in daily life will make a difference. Make sure you never release any pets you may have into the wild. Respect laws about invasive species when traveling. Most countries have signs at their borders that clearly list items that cannot be taken into the country, such as certain foods, animals, and plants. One of the best ways you can help the blue iguana is to organize fundraising events with your friends. Send the money you raise to a blue iguana conservation group.

Climate change affects all endangered species. Plastic contains toxins that cause land, water, and air pollution, which speeds up climate change. Always recycle plastics so they don't harm the environment.

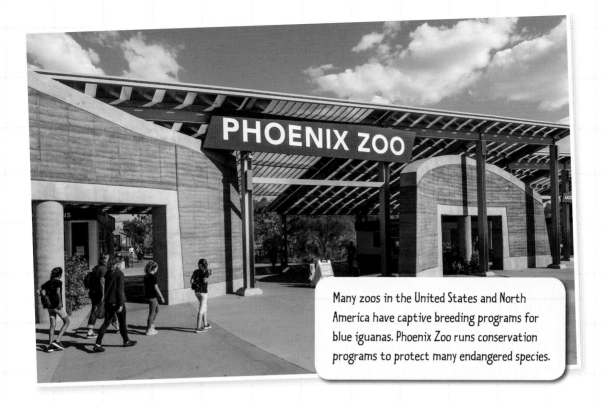

Many zoos in the United States and North America have captive breeding programs for blue iguanas. Phoenix Zoo runs conservation programs to protect many endangered species.

TAKE ACTION AND SPREAD THE WORD

Many people will never see a blue iguana in the wild unless they visit Grand Cayman, but there are still ways you can help them. Sharing information and educating other people is a great start.

- Write a biography of Fred Burton. In your report, explain how he made a difference and saved the blue iguana population.

- Find out if your local zoo supports blue iguanas on Grand Cayman and, if so, ask if there are ways you can become involved as a volunteer.

- Many people have never heard of blue iguanas. Write a story for your local newspaper or community magazine, explaining the main actions that helped the blue iguana come back from the brink of extinction.

- Visit the websites of the conservation organizations and parks mentioned in this book. Follow them on social media for the latest updates on the blue iguana, and share the posts with your friends.

Learning More

Books

Burton, Frederic. *The Little Blue Book: A Short History of the Grand Cayman Blue Iguana.* International Reptile Conservation Foundation, 2010.

Connors, Kathleen. *Iguanas.* (Really Wild Reptiles). Gareth Stevens Publishing, 2014.

Hansen, Grace. *Iguanas.* (Reptiles). Abdo, 2017.

Townsend, Wendy. *Blue Iguana.* Namelos, 2014.

On the Web

www.zoosociety.org/MultiMedia/Stories/BlueIguana.php
Read the story of Joan Maurer, a blue iguana volunteer.

www.youtube.com/watch?v=ORhGANLZzH4&feature=youtu.be
See this Bronx Zoo video of a blue iguana in captivity.

www.youtube.com/watch?time_continue=4&v=fVTsvkHczio
Watch a video from the Department of the Environment Cayman Islands Government showing the differences between green iguanas and blue iguanas.

www.nationalgeographic.com.au/videos/wild-islands/the-blue-iguana-3699.aspx
Watch a blue iguana turn blue in this National Geographic video that shows the early captive breeding center set up by Frederic Burton.

Glossary

bacteria Microscopic organisms that can cause infection

camouflage The color or pattern of an animal's skin or coat to look like its surroundings to hide it from predators

census A count of the number of a species in an area

crest A comb-like ridge on the top of a bird or other animal

cull When wild animals are killed in an organized way

dispersal When something is spread over a large area

downgraded Less serious than before

ecosystem Everything that exists in a particular environment, including animals and plants and nonliving things, such as soil and sunlight

enclosure An area surrounded by fences or another secure barrier

extinct Describes a situation in which all members of a species have died, so the species no longer exists

facility A place equipped for a particular purpose

feral Animals that were once pets but now live in the wild

fragmented When a natural habitat is split up or separated by human or natural habitat destruction

functionally extinct A species with such a small population that it plays no role in the ecosystem and will probably die out

genetic diversity When a species has a variety of genes in its population

habitat The conditions in which an animal or plant naturally lives

hatchling An animal that has just hatched from an egg

herbivore Having a plant-based diet

incubators Equipment where the environment is controlled, such as when hatching eggs

juveniles Young, not fully grown

native species A species that naturally occurs in a particular place

natural scientist A scientist who studies the physical world and its phenomena

predators Animals that hunt other animals for food

reserves Areas of land that are protected and kept wild

roadkill Animals killed by traffic

scales Small, overlapping plates of skin that protect reptiles and fish

species A group of similar animals or plants that can breed with one another

volunteer A person who works for free

Index and About the Author

ABOUT THE AUTHOR

Ruth Daly has over 25 years teaching experience, mainly in elementary schools, and she currently teaches Grade 3. She has written more than 45 non-fiction books for the education market on a wide range of subjects and for a variety of age groups. These include books on animals, life cycles, and the natural environment. Her fiction and poetry have been published in magazines and literary journals. She enjoys travel, reading, and photography, particularly nature and wildlife.